3 Trace the words below. Pay special attention to the letters in color.

5 points per question

(1) hog   log

(2) dog   fog

(3) hot   pot

(4) box   ox

(5) job   sob

(6) hop   mop

4 Connect each word below to the word that rhymes with it. 5 points per question

(1)
job

ⓐ
sob

(2)
ox

ⓑ
dot

(3)
dog

ⓒ
box

(4)
pot

ⓓ
log

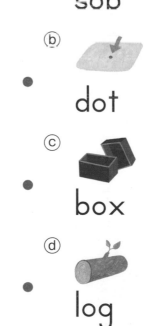

You got it!

1 Trace the words below. Pay special attention to the letters in color.

5 points per question

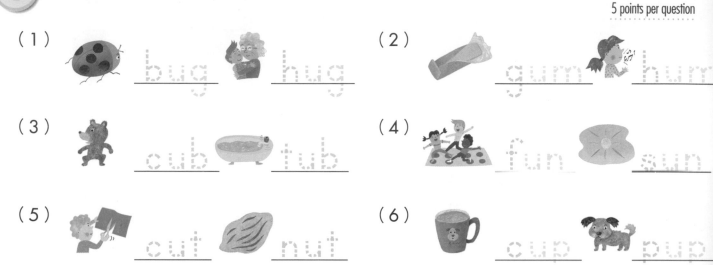

(1) bug hug

(2) gum hum

(3) cub tub

(4) fun sun

(5) cut nut

(6) cup pup

2 Connect each word below to the word that rhymes with it. 5 points per question

(1) gum

(2) nut

(3) cub

(4) sun

ⓐ cut

ⓑ run

ⓒ sub

ⓓ hum

3 Write the correct rhyming word next to each word below. 4 points per question

dot	sub	rat	pit	hen

(1) cat _____   (2) men _____   (3) hit _____

(4) hot _____   (5) tub _____

4 Write the correct word below each picture. 5 points per question

hog	pit	bug	wet	fat	rip
rug	rat	net	sip	fog	hit

(1)

fat _____   _____

(2)

_____   _____

(3)

_____   _____

(4)

_____   _____

(5)

_____   _____

(6)

_____   rug

These pairs all rhyme!

© Kumon Publishing Co., Ltd.   7

1 Trace or write the word that rhymes with the first.
Use the pictures as hints.

4 points per question

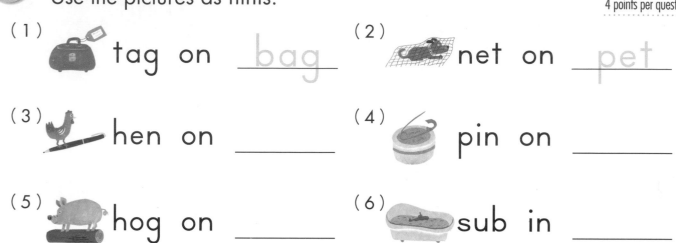

(1) tag on bag

(2) net on pet

(3) hen on _____

(4) pin on _____

(5) hog on _____

(6) sub in _____

2 Finish each word based on the pictures below.

4 points per question

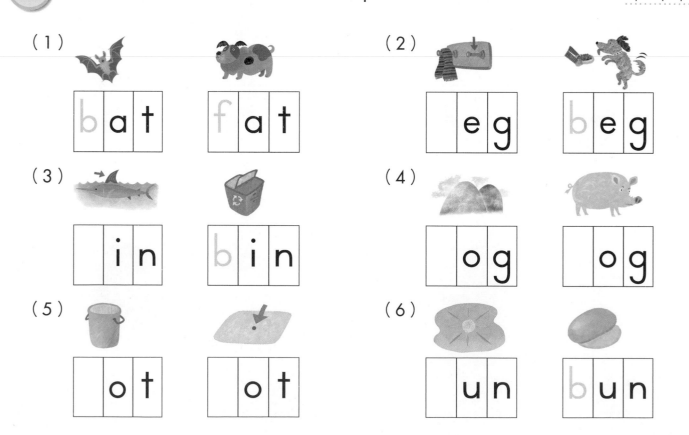

(1) b a t   f a t

(2) e g   b e g

(3) i n   b i n

(4) o g   o g

(5) o t   o t

(6) u n   b u n

3 Trace or write the correct vowels to finish each pair of words below.

4 points per question

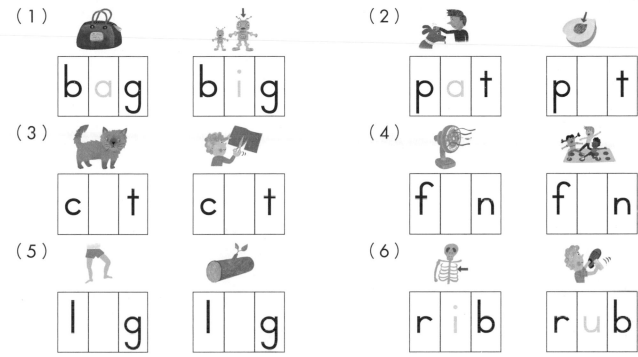

(1)

b	a	g

b	i	g

(2)

p	a	t

p		t

(3)

c		t

c		t

(4)

f		n

f		n

(5)

l		g

l		g

(6)

r	i	b

r	u	b

4 Connect each word to the correct picture below.

4 points per question

(1) hat •

(2) hit •

(3) dig •

(4) log •

(5) cut •

(6) bad •

(7) web •

• ⓐ

• ⓑ

• ⓒ

• ⓓ

• ⓔ

• ⓕ

• ⓖ

Not bad!

Short Vowels Review

Level ☆

Date   /   /

Name

Score   /100

1 Write the correct word below each picture.

3 points per question

(1)

_____

(2)

_____

(3)

_____

(4)

_____

(5)

_____

(6)

_____

(7)

_____

(8)

_____

(9)

_____

(10)

_____

(11)

_____

(12)

_____

2 Complete each rhyming phrase using a word from the box. 8 points per question

| men   cat   log |

(1) <u>cat</u> on mat

(2) ten _____ sit

(3) dog on _____

3 Draw a line from the arrow (➡) to the star (★) by connecting only words with the short 'a' sound, like 'bag' and 'cat.'

gum	big	hog	lid	bat
dig	mud	log	rag	bag
pig	sit	hen	rat	bed
hug	peg	pen	mat	red
lip	mad	pan	man	hit
wig	bad	dot	pin	set
jet	cab	pet	pit	pot
hat	nap	net	cut	leg

★

That was fun!

Consonant Combinations
bl, cl, fl, pl

Level ★★

Score /100

Date / /

Name

1 Trace the words below.

3 points per question

(1) block

(2) blast

(3) clap

(4) climb

(5) flag

(6) float

(7) plant

(8) plum

2 Connect each word to the correct picture below.

4 points per question

(1) clap •

(2) black •

(3) climb •

(4) class •

(5) plum •

(6) blast •

• ⓐ

• ⓑ

• ⓒ

• ⓓ

• ⓔ

• ⓕ

3 Write each word below. Use the pictures as hints.

(1)

_____

(2)

_____

(3)

_____

(4)

_____

(5)

_____

(6)

_____

(7)

<u>clock</u>

(8)

<u>flat</u>

4 Complete each phrase using a word from the box below. Use the pictures as hints.

block	clap	flag	clock

(1)

clean _____

(2)

black _____

(3)

_____ in class

(4)

fly the _____

Blam! You did it!

Consonant Combinations
br, cr, fr, gr

7

Level ⭐⭐

Date / /

Name

Score /100

1 Trace the words below.

4 points per question

(1)

b̶r̶i̶c̶k̶

(2)

b̶r̶a̶g̶

(3)

c̶r̶y̶

(4)

c̶r̶a̶b̶

(5)

f̶r̶o̶g̶

(6)

f̶r̶o̶n̶t̶

(7)

g̶r̶a̶s̶s̶

(8)

g̶r̶a̶b̶

2 Connect each word to the correct picture below.

4 points per question

(1) brag •

• ⓐ

(2) brown•

• ⓑ

(3) cry •

• ⓒ

(4) crib •

• ⓓ

(5) front •

• ⓔ

(6) grass •

• ⓕ

3 Write each word below. Use the pictures as hints.

4 points per question

(1)

_____

(2)

_____

(3)

_____

(4)

_____

(5)

_____

(6)

_____

4 Complete each phrase using a word from the box below. Use the pictures as hints.

5 points per question

frog	brick	crib	grass

(1)

_____ in front

(2)

brown _____

(3)

cry in the _____

(4)

grab the _____

Well done!

Consonant Combinations
sk, sm, sn, sp

Level
★★

Date
/ /

Name

Score
/100

1 Trace the words below.

4 points per question

(1) sky

(2)  skin

(3) small

(4)  smell

(5) snow

(6) snake

(7) spot

(8) spin

2 Connect each word to the correct picture below.

4 points per question

(1) sky •

• ⓐ

(2) spot •

• ⓑ

(3) snake•

• ⓒ

(4) small •

• ⓓ

(5) skirt •

• ⓔ

(6) skip •

• ⓕ

3 Write each word below. Use the pictures as hints.

4 points per question

(1)

_____

(2)

_____

(3)

_____

(4)

_____

(5)

_____

(6)

_____

4 Complete each phrase using a word from the box below. Use the pictures as hints.

5 points per question

| smell | skip | spy | snake |

(1)

spin a ___spy___

(2)

small _____

(3)

_____ in skirt

(4)

_____ in snow

You got it.

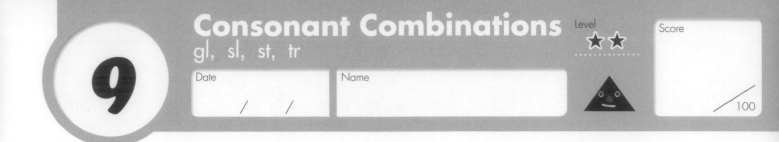

Consonant Combinations
gl, sl, st, tr

1 Trace the words below.

4 points per question

(1)  <u>glass</u>

(2)  <u>glad</u>

(3)  <u>sleep</u>

(4)  <u>slow</u>

(5)  <u>star</u>

(6)  <u>step</u>

(7) <u>tree</u>

(8) <u>trip</u>

2 Connect each word to the correct picture below.

4 points per question

(1) **star** (2) **sleep** (3) **tree** (4) **stick** (5) **start** (6) **slip**

ⓐ  ⓑ  ⓒ  ⓓ  ⓔ  ⓕ

3 Write each word below. Use the pictures as hints.

4 points per question

(1)  _____

(2) _____

(3) _____

(4)  _____

(5)  _____

(6)  _____

4 Complete each phrase using a word from the box below. Use the pictures as hints.

5 points per question

slip	step	glass	tree

(1) one _____ to start

(2) glad for a _____

(3) slow down, don't _____

(4) trip to _____

You are a star!

Consonant Combinations
-nt, -mp, -nk, -st

Level ★ ★

Date / /

Name

Score / 100

 1 Trace the words below.

4 points per question

(1) ant

(2)  tent

(3) jump

(4) lamp

(5) bank

(6) ink

(7) best

(8)  fast

2 Connect each word to the correct picture below.

4 points per question

(1) ink •

• ⓐ

(2) best •

• ⓑ

(3) ant •

• ⓒ

(4) tent •

• ⓓ

(5) sink •

• ⓔ

(6) bump •

• ⓕ

Write each word below. Use the pictures as hints.

(1)

_____

(2)

_____

(3)

_____

(4)

_____

(5)

_____

(6)

_____

4 Complete each phrase using a word from the box below.
Use the pictures as hints.

fast	tent	ink	jump

(1) ant in _____

(2) _____ on bump

(3) _____ in sink

(4) best and _____

You are fast!

11

Consonant Combinations
wh, sh, ch, th

Date   /   /

Name

Level ★★

Score /100

---

1   Trace the words below.

3 points per question

(1)  *what*

(2) *wheel*

(3) *sheep*

(4) *shark*

(5) *chin*

(6) *chop*

(7) *thin*

(8) *thick*

---

2   Connect each word to the correct picture below.

4 points per question

(1) wheel •

(2) ship •

(3) thin •

(4) shirt •

(5) chop •

(6) chair •

(7) three •

(8) chin •

• ⓐ

• ⓑ

• ⓒ

• ⓓ

• ⓔ

• ⓕ

• ⓖ

• ⓗ **3...**

---

22   © Kumon Publishing Co., Ltd.

3 Write each word below. Use the pictures as hints.

4 points per question

(1)

_____

(2)

_____

(3)

_____

(4)

_____

(5)

_____

(6)

3...

_____

4 Complete each phrase using a word from the box below. Use the pictures as hints.

5 points per question

thin   wheel   sheep   chair

(1) where is the _____

(2) the _____ man

(3) child on _____

(4) _____ on ship

You are sharp!

12

Consonant Combinations
-sh, -ch, -nd, -ck

Level ★★

Date   /   /

Name

Score

/100

1 Trace the words below.

3 points per question

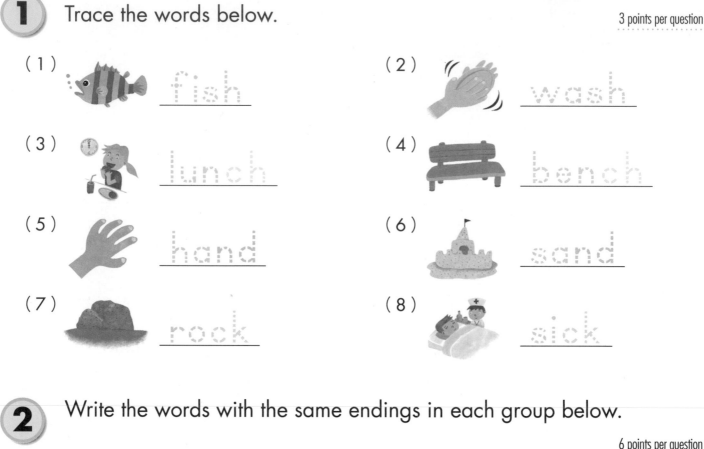

(1) fish

(2) wash

(3) lunch

(4) bench

(5) hand

(6) sand

(7) rock

(8) sick

2 Write the words with the same endings in each group below.

6 points per question

| fish | rock | hand | kick | sock | lunch |
| band | bunch | dish | bench | wish | sand |

(1) ends in "sh"

fish _____ _____

(2) ends in "ch"

lunch _____ _____

(3) ends in "nd"

hand _____ _____

(4) ends in "ck"

rock _____ _____

3 Write each word below. Use the pictures as hints.

(1) _____

(2) _____

(3) _____

(4) _____

(5) _____

(6) dish

(7) band

(8) sock

4 Complete each phrase using a word from the box below. Use the pictures as hints.

5 points per question

fish	rock	lunch	hand

(1) _____ on dish

(2) _____ on bench

(3) _____ in sand

(4) sock on _____

You rock!

25

Consonant Combinations Review

Level ★★

Date   /   /

Name

Score   /100

1 Circle the word that matches the picture.

3 points per question

(1)   class   glass   camp   clock

(2)   drink   dig   dog   ink

(3)   chop   spin   chin   cat

(4)   think   three   trip   moth

(5)   hand   sand   top   sit

2 Pick the correct word from the box to match each picture below.

6 points per question

| wheel | dish | hand | kick | grass | tent |

(1) _____

(2) _____

(3) _____

(4) _____

(5) _____

(6) _____

3 Draw a line to match each phrase on the left to the correct picture on the right.

4 points per question

(1) best and last •

(2) block on truck •

(3) hand with sand •

(4) fish on dish •

(5) shirt in wash •

(6) sheep on ship •

ⓐ •

ⓑ •

ⓒ •

ⓓ •

ⓔ •

ⓕ •

4 Complete each phrase using a word from the box below. Use the pictures as hints.

5 points per question

| lunch | front | sand | bump | clock |

(1) clean the _____

(2) pond and _____

(3) _____ on bench

(4) frog in _____

(5) jump on _____

You are good!
Keep it up!

27

14

Long Vowels
'a' Sounds

Date

Name

Level ★ ★

Score

/100

1 Say the words aloud. Then trace the letters.

2 points per question

(1)

cane

(2)

mane

(3)

lane

(4)

plane

(5)

play

(6)

day

(7)

bay

(8)

hay

(9)

rain

(10)

pain

(11)

brain

(12)

train

2 Connect each word to the correct picture below.

2 points per question

(1) **mane** •

(2) **cake** •

(3) **lake** •

(4) **hay** •

(5) **pay** •

(6) **rain** •

(7) **pail** •

(8) **mail** •

ⓐ

ⓑ

ⓒ

ⓓ

ⓔ

ⓕ

ⓖ

ⓗ

3 Pick the correct word from the box to match each picture below.

4 points per question

lane	day	cane	train	pail	cake
cape	pay	pain	paint		

(1) _____

(2) _____

(3) _____

(4) _____

(5) _____

(6) _____

(7) _____

(8) _____

(9) _____

(10) _____

4 Complete each phrase using a word from the box below.
Use the pictures as hints.

5 points per question

plane	rain	play	hay

(1) cane on _____

(2) _____ by the bay

(3) play by the _____

(4) _____ on the train

You get an `a´!
Well done.

29

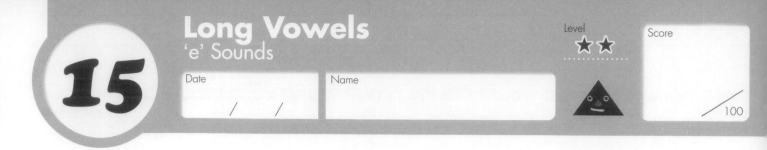

Long Vowels
'e' Sounds

15

Level ★★

Date   /   /

Name

Score
        /100

1 Help the lost bee find his tree! Say the words aloud as you trace them.

2 points per question

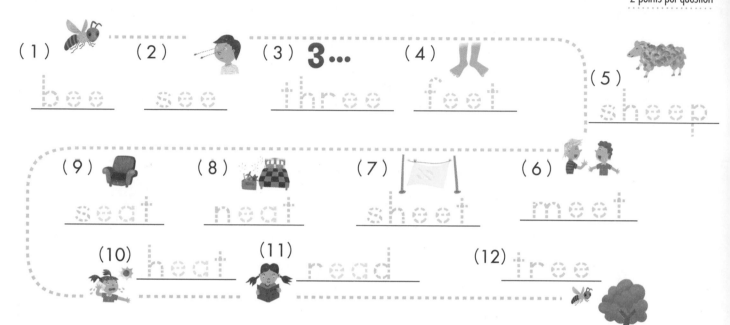

(1) bee   (2) see   (3) **3...** three   (4) feet   (5) sheep

(9) seat   (8) neat   (7) sheet   (6) meet

(10) heat   (11) read   (12) tree

2 Connect each word to the correct picture below.

2 points per question

(1) bee •

(2) read •

(3) street •

(4) feet •

(5) tea •

(6) deep •

(7) clean •

(8) pea •

ⓐ •

ⓑ •

ⓒ •

ⓓ •

ⓔ •

ⓕ •

ⓖ •

ⓗ •

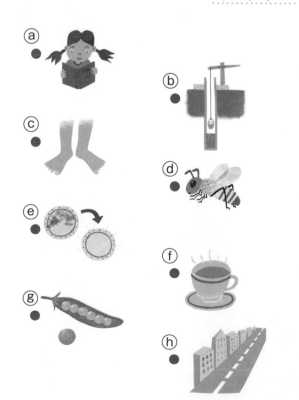

3 Pick the correct word from the box to match each picture below.

3 points per question

sheep	neat	bee	meet	heat	tree
three	seat	see	read	feet	sheet

(1) _____

(2) _____

(3) _____

(4) **3···** _____

(5) _____

(6) _____

(7) _____

(8) _____

(9) _____

(10) _____

(11) _____

(12) _____

4 Complete each phrase using a word from the box below.
Use the pictures as hints.

6 points per question

tree	sheet	eat	read

(1) sheep eats the _____

(2) see the _____

(3) _____ in the heat

(4) _____ on seat

Now you see! Good!

Long Vowels
'i' Sounds

1 Say the words aloud. Then trace the letters.

2 points per question

(1)

sky

(2)

fly

(3)

cry

(4)

dry

(5)

kite

(6)

bite

(7)

hike

(8)

bike

(9)

hide

(10)

ride

(11)

slide

(12)

wide

2 Circle the correct word for each picture below.

5 points per question

(1) kite   hide   kit   bit

(2) rid   ride   rib   cry

(3) fly   fire   fine   fin

(4) slide   kite   bite   smile

3 Pick the correct word from the box to match each picture below.

3 points per question

cry	dry	wide	hide	hike	bite
five	fly	slide	kite	sky	ride

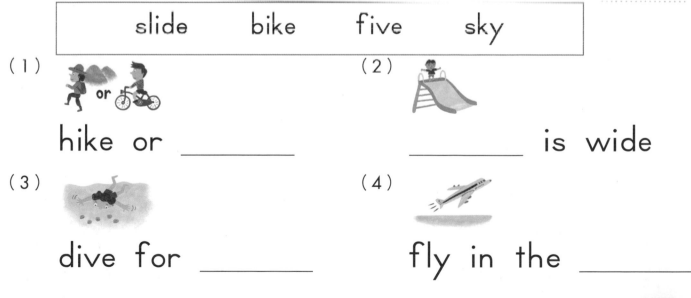

(1) _____

(2) _____

(3) _____

(4) _____

(5) _____

(6) _____

(7) _____

(8) **5.....** _____

(9) _____

(10) _____

(11) _____

(12) _____

4 Complete each phrase using a word from the box below.
Use the pictures as hints.

5 points per question

slide	bike	five	sky

(1) hike or _____

(2) _____ is wide

(3) dive for _____

(4) fly in the _____

You are doing fine!

17

Long Vowels
'o' Sounds

Level ★★

Score /100

Date   /   /

Name

1 What a funny pair! Trace each pair of words and say them aloud.

4 points per question

(1) cone and bone

(2) coat and goat

(3) hose and rose

(4) float and boat

(5) nose and close

(6) toad and road

2 Connect each word to the correct picture below.

4 points per question

(1) close •

(2) boat •

(3) cone •

(4) road •

(5) float •

(6) hose •

(7) hole •

(8) rope •

ⓐ •

ⓑ •

ⓒ •

ⓓ •

ⓔ •

ⓕ •

ⓖ •

ⓗ •

3 Pick the correct word from the box to match each picture below.

2 points per question

float	coat	hole	bone	toad	goat
road	rose	boat	cone	nose	rope

(1) _____

(2) _____

(3) _____

(4) _____

(5) _____

(6) _____

(7) _____

(8) _____

(9) _____

(10) _____

(11) _____

(12) _____

4 Complete each phrase using a word from the box below.
Use the pictures as hints.

4 points per question

nose	boat	coat	toad	rose

(1) _____ on a goat

(2) _____ can float

(3) hose and _____

(4) close your _____

(5) _____ on the road

You have a nose for this!

Long Vowels
'u' Sounds

Level ★ ★

Date / / 　Name

Score /100

---

1 Say the words aloud. Then trace the letters.

3 points per question

(1)
cube

(2)
tube

(3)
cute

(4)
flute

(5)
tune

(6)
dune

(7)
blue

(8)
glue

---

2 Circle the correct word for each picture below.

5 points per question

(1)　cute　　flute　　cut　　sub

(2)　cube　　cub　　rule　　cute

(3)　bun　　tune　　tub　　tube

(4)　tin　　tune　　tube　　dune

36　© Kumon Publishing Co., Ltd.

3 Pick the correct word from the box to match each picture below.

4 points per question

| cube | blue | cute | tune |
| dune | flute | tube | glue |

(1)

_____

(2)

_____

(3)

_____

(4)

_____

(5)

_____

(6)

_____

(7)

_____

(8)

_____

4 Complete each phrase using a word from the box below.
Use the pictures as hints.

6 points per question

| dune | flute | glue | cube |

(1) tune on the _____

(2) use blue _____

(3) cute _____

(4) _____ and tube

Don't be blue.
You can do it!

19 Long Vowels Review

Level

Date / /

Name

Score

/100

1 Pick the correct word from the box to match each picture below.

3 points per question

bay	bee	boat	ride	cane	make
blue	sky	glue	mail	cone	clean

(1)

make

(2)
_____

(3)
_____

(4)
_____

(5)
_____

(6)
_____

(7)
_____

(8)
_____

(9)
_____

(10)
_____

(11)
_____

(12)
_____

2 Complete each phrase using a word from the box below.
Use the pictures as hints.

6 points per question

slide	rain	float	feet

(1) _____ on the street

(2) train in the _____

(3) hide by the _____

(4) coat will _____

3 Draw a line from the arrow (➡) to the star (★) by connecting only words with the long 'a' sound, like 'gate' and 'mail.'

40 points for completion

hot	ride	name	date	gate
net	rope	nail	dam	kite
pot	rain	mail	maid	paid
pet	can	man	jam	page
plate	lake	cave	pan	cage
plane	bat	wave	bake	cake
cane	hole	pea	meet	make
tail	mole	sea	home	dine

★

That was fun!

Long Vowels Review

Date / /

Name

Score /100

1 Find and circle the words from the box in the groups of letters below.

4 points per question

| road   sheet   blue   hike   meat |

(1) y k h i k e m p q t

(2) z n t h i b l u e y x

(3) r t m e a t b i d z u

(4) o p r d y r o a d w q s

(5) s q m d l s h e e t r t y

2 Fill in the missing vowels.

6 points per question

(1) p l n

(2) s l p

(3) b t

(4) g t

3 Pick the correct word from the box to match each picture below.

3 points per question

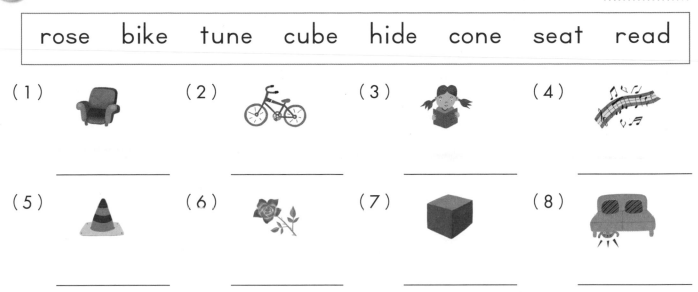

| rose | bike | tune | cube | hide | cone | seat | read |

(1) _____

(2) _____

(3) _____

(4) _____

(5) _____

(6) _____

(7) _____

(8) _____

4 Finish each sentence below. Use the pictures as hints.

8 points per question

(1) The glue is _____ .

(2) The _____ can float.

(3) I _____ and smile.

(4) We eat _____ at the lake.

Smile! You are doing well!

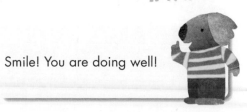

Vocabulary
Numbers

Date / /

Name

Level ★ ★

Score / 100

1 Trace the words after looking at the dots below.

2 points per question

(1) ●   one

(2) ●●   two

(3) ●●●   three

(4) ●●●●   four

(5) ●●●●●   five

(6) ●●●●● ●   six

(7) ●●●●● ●●   seven

2 Count the objects. Then write the word for the correct number of objects below.

3 points per question

(1)

_____

(2)

_____

(3)

_____

(4)

_____

(5)

_____

(6)

_____

(7)

_____

(8)

_____

(9)

_____

(10)

_____

(11)

_____

(12)

_____

3 Connect each sentence to the correct picture on the right.   6 points per question

(1) Three cats sleep. •

(2) One plane lands. •

(3) Seven bugs fly. •

(4) Two frogs jump. •

(5) Six dogs run. •

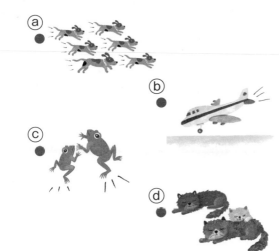

4 Color the picture after reading each sentence below.   5 points per question

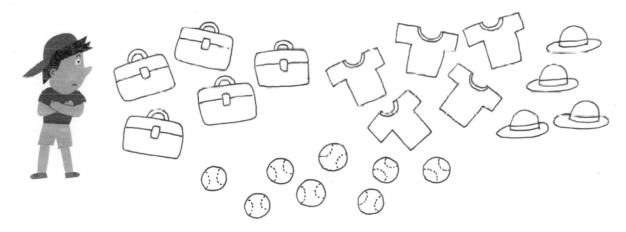

(1) Color **four** bags.

(2) Color **three** shirts.

(3) Color **two** hats.

(4) Color **five** balls.

Now you can read numbers! Good job.

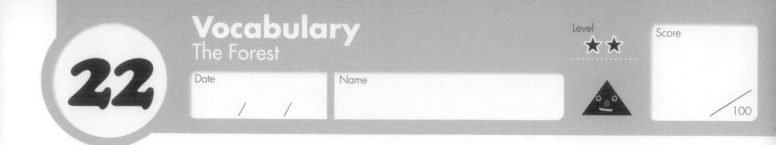

Vocabulary
The Forest

Date   /   /

Name

Level
★ ★

Score

/100

22

1 Trace the words shown in the forest below.

2 points per question

(1) wind

(2) leaf

(3) jump

(4) catch

(5) bird

(6) climb

(7) water

(8) wolf

2 Trace and write the following words. Use the pictures as hints.

3 points per question

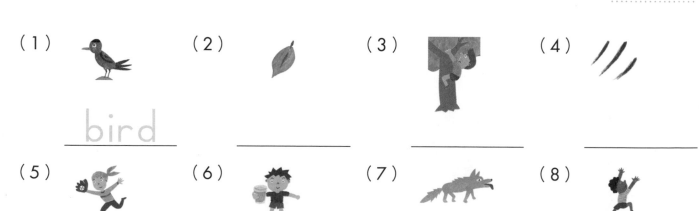

(1)   (2)   (3)   (4)

bird

(5)   (6)   (7)   (8)

3 Look at the picture. Then write the correct letter for each sentence below.

5 points per question

(1) The boat is in the water. ( )

(2) Three birds fly. ( )

(3) The wind is strong. ( )

(4) The tea is hot. ( )

4 Finish each sentence with the correct word from the box.

8 points per question

jump	catch	wolf	wind	bird

(1) The _____ has two wings and a tail.

(2) Can you _____ rope?

(3) I like to play _____ in the park.

(4) The park zoo has a big, gray _____.

(5) I fly my kite in the _____.

Do you like to hike in the forest?

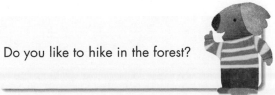

23

Vocabulary
The Classroom

Date   /   /

Name

Level ★★

Score

        /100

1 Trace the words shown in the classroom below.

2 points per question

(1) watch

(2) make

(3) glue

(4) string

(5) sing

(6) chair

(7) read

(8) desk

2 Write the following words. Use the pictures as hints.

3 points per question

(1)

(2)

(3)

(4)

_____

_____

_____

_____

(5)

(6)

(7)

(8)

_____

_____

_____

_____

3 Finish each sentence with the correct word from the box. 8 points per question

read	sing	watch	chair	make

(1) I _____ my book in class.

(2) My _____ has four legs.

(3) We _____ a song about the flag.

(4) My _____ tells time.

(5) I like to _____ things with string.

4 Read the sentences below. Circle the "**T**" if the sentence is true, or correct. Circle the "**F**" if the sentence is false, or wrong. 5 points per question

True is correct!
False is wrong!

(1) There are five plants on the big desk. **T** **F**

(2) The string is on top of the drum. **T** **F**

(3) The fish is in the sea. **T** **F**

(4) The man in blue reads the book. **T** **F**

You are the best in the class!

Vocabulary
The Pet Store

24

Date   /   /

Name

Level ★★★

Score /100

1 Trace the words shown in the pet store below.

2 points per question

(1) frog

(2) rabbit

(3) snake

(4) dog

(5) bat

(6) ant

(7) fish

(8) cat

2 Write the following words. Use the pictures as hints.

3 points per question

(1)
_____

(2)
_____

(3)
_____

(4)
_____

(5)
_____

(6)
_____

(7)
_____

(8)
_____

3 Finish each sentence with the correct word from the box.

6 points per question

| dog | snake | fish | cat | ant |

(1) My _____ likes to bark.

(2) The _____ drinks milk.

(3) The _____ is long.

(4) My _____ swims in his tank.

(5) I saw an _____ climb the wall.

4 Finish each sentence below. Use the picture as a hint.

6 points per question

(1) The boy in red has a _____.

(2) A _____ is out of his cage!

(3) The snake is on the _____ farm.

(4) The _____ is very scared.

(5) The _____ is happy in his tank.

This is fun! Keep it up.

25

Vocabulary
Adjectives

Date   /   /

Name

Level ★★★

Score

/100

1 Trace the words below.

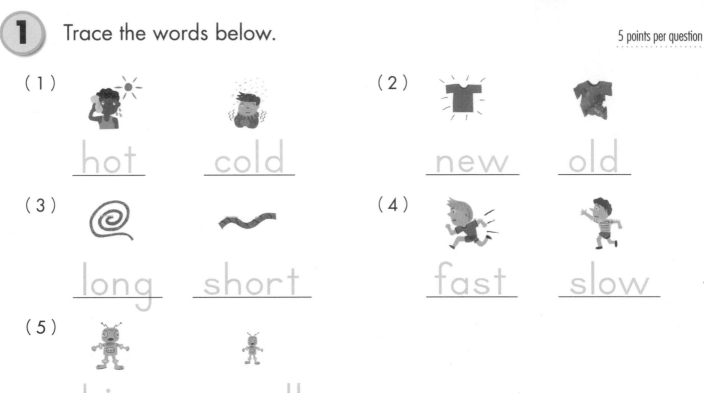

(1)

hot   cold

(2)

new   old

(3)

long   short

(4)

fast   slow

(5)

big   small

2 Finish each sentence with the correct word from the box.

fast   cold   old   new   long

(1) The watch is _____ .

(2) The snake is _____ .

(3) The water feels _____ .

(4) The wolf runs _____ .

(5) The man is _____ .

3 Circle the correct picture for each sentence below.

5 points per question

(1) The drink is cold.

(2) The ball is too far to catch.

(3) The fast car wins the race.

(4) The short dog jumps.

4 Draw a line between the words that mean the **opposite**.

6 points per question

(1) hot •

(2) old •

(3) short •

(4) slow •

(5) big •

• ⓐ small

• ⓑ new

• ⓒ fast

• ⓓ cold

• ⓔ long

You are fast, not slow!

51

Vocabulary
Directions

26

Date / /

Name

Level ★★★

Score

/100

1 Trace the words below.

5 points per question

(1)

left   right

(2)

stop   go

(3)

near   far

(4)

up   down

2 Write the following words. Use the pictures as hints.

3 points per question

(1)

_____

(2)

_____

(3)

_____

(4)

_____

(5)

_____

(6)

_____

(7)

_____

(8)

_____

(9)

_____

(10)

_____

(11)

_____

(12)

_____

3 Circle the correct picture for each sentence below.

5 points per question

(1) The car stops.

(2) The car turns right.

(3) The car drives down the hill.

(4) The car is far.

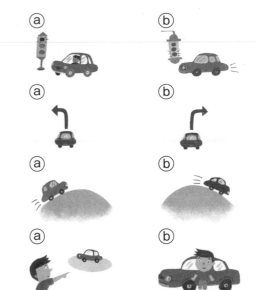

4 Start at the dot and draw a line to find the treasure.

6 points per question

(1) Turn left at the tree.

(2) Go up the hill.

(3) Stop at the white bench.

(4) Go to the box near the frog.

You found the gold! Good job!

27

Level
★★★

Date / /

Name

Score
/100

---

1 Read the passage. Then finish the sentences below to match the passage.

15 points per question

> A fox saw a bunch of grapes.
> The grapes were big and red.
> They smelled sweet.
> The fox liked fruit.
> He liked apples.
> He liked plums.

---

(1) The grapes were big and _____.

(2) The grapes smelled _____.

(3) The _____ liked fruit.

(4) The fox liked _____ and plums.

2 Read the passage. Then match the sentences to the pictures below by writing the letter of the sentence next to the correct picture.   8 points per question

The fox wanted to eat the grapes.
He liked grape jam.   ⋯ a
He liked grape pie.   ⋯ b
He liked grape cake.   ⋯ c
He liked grapes with apples. ⋯ d
He liked grape drink.   ⋯ e
He liked all kinds of grapes.

(1)

grape pie

(b)

(2)

jam

( )

(3)

( )

(4)

( )

(5)

( )

Do you like grapes?

Reading Comprehension
The Fox and the Grapes 2

28

Level

Score
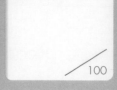
/100

Date   /   /   Name

1 Read the passage. Then read the sentences below. Circle the "**T**" if the sentence is true, or correct. Circle the "**F**" if the sentence is false, or wrong.

10 points per question

> The grapes were on a vine.
> The vine was thick and green.
> The fox was short.
> The vine was tall.
> The short fox looked up.
> The best grapes were on top of the vine.

(1) The vine was green.   **T** **F**

(2) The fox was short.   **T** **F**

(3) The fox was tall.   **T** **F**

(4) The fox looked down.   **T** **F**

(5) The fox looked up.   **T** **F**

2 Read the passage. Then number the pictures below to match the same order as the passage.

50 points for completion

The fox ran.

The fox jumped.

The fox missed.

The grapes were too far.

The fox was mad.

The fox left.

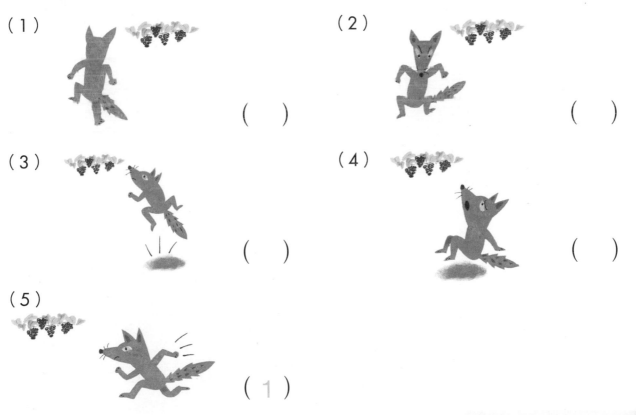

(1)   (   )

(2)   (   )

(3)   (   )

(4)   (   )

(5)   (1)

You can read really well!

Reading Comprehension
Rip and Spot 1

29

Level
★★★

Date
/   /

Name

Score

/100

1 Read the passage. Then finish the sentences below to match the passage.

15 points per question

I am Rip.

My hair is short.

My watch is new.

This is Spot.

Spot is my dog.

His spot is black.

We run in the park.

I am Rip.

I am Spot.

(1) Rip has short _____.

(2) Rip has a _____ watch.

(3) Spot has a _____ spot.

(4) Rip and Spot _____ in the park.

2 Read the passage. Then match the sentences to the pictures below by writing the letter of the sentence next to the correct picture.

8 points per question

> We run in the park. ··· a
> We see birds in a tree. ··· b
> We fish at the beach. ··· c
> We climb up rocks. ··· d
> Spot, let's run up that hill. ··· e
> You run fast, Spot. You win! ··· f
> Let's get water to drink. ··· g
> I see a stream. ··· h

(1)

(c)

(2)

( )

(3)

( )

(4)

( )

(5)

( )

You can read fast!

Reading Comprehension
Rip and Spot 2

30

Level

Score

Date
/ /

Name

/100

1 Read the passage. Then read the sentences below. Circle the "**T**" if the sentence is true, or correct. Circle the "**F**" if the sentence is false, or wrong.

8 points per question

This is a big stream.

Can we drink the water?

The water is not too hot or too cold.

This water is just right.

I am hot. I am tired. I want to sleep.

Let's take a nap by that small, green tree.

---

(1) The stream is small.   T   F

(2) The water is too hot.   T   F

(3) Rip is cold.   T   F

(4) Rip wants to sleep.   T   F

(5) The tree is small and green.   T   F

2 Read the passage. Then number the pictures to match the same order as the passage.

60 points for completion

Wake up, Spot!
This tree is not the same.
This tree is big.
Ouch! My back hurts!
Spot, your spot is gray! You are old!
My hair is long and gray! I am old!
Where is my watch?
How long did we sleep?
Let's run home.

(1) (   )

(2) (   )

(3) My back! (   )

(4) (   )

(5) (1)

(6) (   )

You can read big words!

31

Date / /

Name

1 Read the passage. Then read the sentences below. Circle the "**T**" if the sentence is true, or correct. Circle the "**F**" if the sentence is false, or wrong.

8 points per question

> Three pigs wanted safe homes.
>
> One pig made a home from hay.
>
> It was quick to make.
>
> One pig made a home from sticks.
>
> It was quick to make.
>
> One pig made a home from bricks.
>
> It was not quick to make.

(1) Five pigs wanted homes. **T   F**

(2) The pigs made homes. **T   F**

(3) One home was made from hay. **T   F**

(4) The stick home was quick to make. **T   F**

(5) The brick home was quick to make. **T   F**

2 Read the passage. Then answer the questions using words from the box.

20 points per question

Then a wolf came.
The wolf went to the hay home.
The wolf said, "I will catch you, pig!"
The pig said, "Not by the hair on my chin!"
The wolf said, "Then I will huff.
I will puff. That home will fall."
The hay home fell.

| pig | hay | chin | hair |

(1) Where did the wolf go?
The wolf went to the _____ home.

(2) Who did the wolf want to catch?
The wolf wanted to catch the _____.

(3) What did the pig say?
The pig said, "Not by the _____ on my _____!"

Help save the pigs from the wolf!

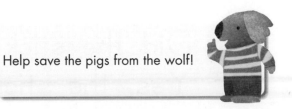

Reading Comprehension
The Three Pigs 2

32

Level

Date / /

Name

Score

/100

1 Read the passage. Then answer the questions using words from the passage.

10 points per question

> The pig ran to the stick home.
> The wolf went to the stick home, too.
> The wolf said, "I will catch you two pigs."
> The two pigs both said, "Not by
> the hair on my chin!"
> The wolf said, "Then I will huff.
> I will puff. That home will fall."
> The stick home fell, too.

(1) Where did the pig run?
The pig ran to the _____ home.

(2) Where did the wolf go?
The wolf went to the _____ home, too.

(3) Who did the wolf want to catch?
The wolf wanted to catch the _____.

(4) Did the stick home fall, too?
Yes, the stick home _____, too.

2 Read the passage. Then number the pictures to match the order in the passage.

60 points for completion

The two pigs ran from the stick home.
The two pigs ran to the brick home.
The wolf went to the brick home, too.
The wolf said, "I will catch all three of you pigs."
The three pigs all said, "Not by the hair on my chin!"
The wolf said, "Then I will huff and puff.
That house will fall."
But the brick home did not fall.
The mad wolf left.

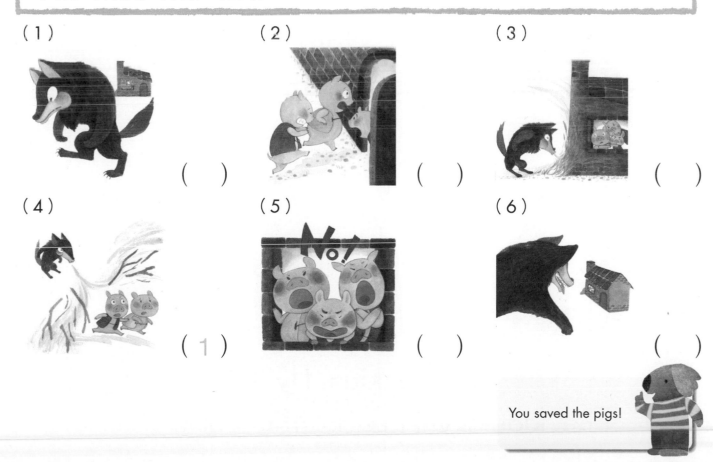

(1)

(2)

(3)

( )

( )

( )

(4)

(5)

(6)

(1)

( )

( )

You saved the pigs!

33

Reading Comprehension
Kate and Kite Day 1

Level ★★★

Date / /

Name

Score /100

1 Read the passage. Then complete the questions using words from the box.

10 points per question

Kite Day is in March.
First all the kids make kites.
Then a band plays.
Then we fly kites in the park.
I like Kite Day.

| Who | What | When | Where |

(1) <u>When</u> is Kite Day?
Kite Day is in March.

(2) _____ makes kites on Kite Day?
All the kids make kites on Kite Day.

(3) _____ does the band do?
The band plays.

(4) _____ do the kids fly kites?
The kids fly kites in the park.

2 Read the passage. Then answer the questions using words from the passage.

15 points per question

We make kites with paper and string.
First I paint my kite pink.
Then I add white stripes.
My name is Kate.
The name "Kate" starts with a "K."
I paint a red "K" on my kite next.

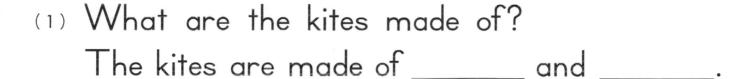

(1) What are the kites made of?
The kites are made of _____ and _____.

(2) What does Kate paint first?
First Kate paints the kite _____.

(3) What does Kate paint next?
Kate paints a _____ "___" next.

(4) Why does Kate paint a "K" on her kite?
The name "Kate" _____ _____ a "K."

Good job!

67

Reading Comprehension
Kate and Kite Day 2

Level ★★★

Date / /

Name

Score /100

1 Read the passage. Then read the sentences below. Circle the **"T"** if the sentence is true, or correct. Circle the **"F"** if the sentence is false, or wrong.

10 points per question

> I put a tail on my kite last.
> I use green cloth for the tail.
> Then I watch the band play.
> I can hear the drum thump.
> The band marches to the park.

(1) Kate makes the tail first.   T   F

(2) Kate uses white cloth for the tail.   T   F

(3) Kate watches the band play.   T   F

(4) Kate hears the drum.   T   F

(5) The band marches to the park.   T   F

2 Read the passage. Then number the pictures to match the order in the passage.

50 points for completion

The band plays a song in the park.
The wind blows in my hair.
I hold my kite by the string.
I run as fast as I can.
My kite jumps up in the wind.
I like Kite Day.

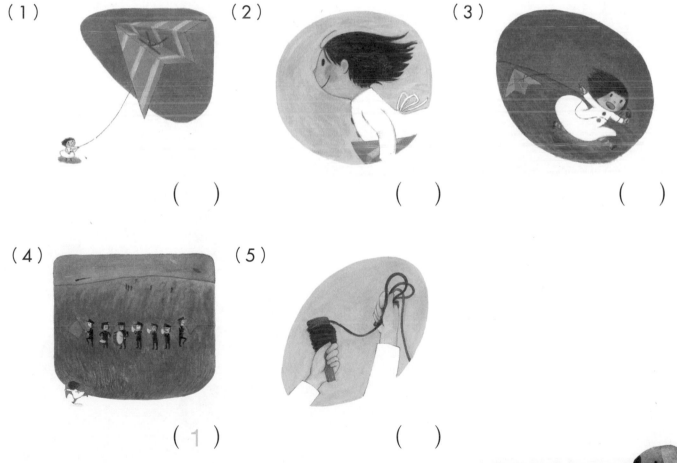

(1)   (   )

(2)   (   )

(3)   (   )

(4)   (1)

(5)   (   )

Wow! You are good!

Date / /

Name

1 Complete the rhyming sentences below. Use the pictures as hints.

5 points per question

(1) Dad is _____ .

(2) The _____ is fat.

(3) The pot is _____ .

(4) We had fun in the _____ .

(5) The bag has a _____ .

2 Connect each word to the correct picture below.

2 points per question

(1) wash •

(2) class •

(3) grab •

(4) thin •

(5) smell •

(6) star •

(7) ink •

(8) wheel •

ⓐ •

ⓑ •

ⓒ •

ⓓ •

ⓔ •

ⓕ •

ⓖ •

ⓗ •

3 Pick the correct word from the box to match each picture below.

4 points per question

sky	tune	pain	bone	read	sheep

(1) _____

(2) _____

(3) _____

(4) _____

(5) _____

(6) _____

4 Complete the sentences using the words in the box below. 7 points per question

lunch	sleep	lake	fast	chair

(1) What did you bring for _____?
I am hungry!

(2) A _____ has four legs and you sit on it.

(3) If I drop a rock in the _____,
it will sink.

(4) I am tired. It is time to _____.

(5) She won the race.
She is _____!

You are close to the end!

Review
Kate and Kite Day 3

36

Level

Score

Date   /   /

Name

/100

1 Read the passage. Then answer the questions below.

One kite gets away!
Where does it go?
It goes up and up and up.
Two kites crash to the grass.
My kite gets tangled with two other kites.
Our three kites are stuck!
We have to take them down.
It is time to go home.
What a fun day!

（1） Answer the questions using words from the passage.   10 points per question

① Where does one kite go?
It goes up and _____ and _____.

② What do the two kites do?
Two kites crash to the _____.

③ What do the three kites do?
The three kites are _____.

（2） Number the pictures in the order of the passage. 35 points for completion

① 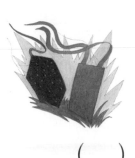 ( )

②  (1)

③  ( )

④ 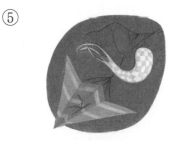 ( )

⑤  ( )

（3） Read the sentences below. Circle the "**T**" if the sentence is true, or correct. Circle the "**F**" if the sentence is false, or wrong. 7 points per question

① One kite gets away. **T** **F**

② Kate's kite crashes to the grass. **T** **F**

③ Kate's kite is stuck. **T** **F**

④ Kate has to take her kite down. **T** **F**

⑤ Kite day is fun. **T** **F**

Wow! You did it!

73

1 Short Vowels   pp 2,3

1
(1) cat, hat   (2) bat, rat
(3) pan, man   (4) can, fan
(5) dad, sad   (6) bag, tag

2
(1) ⓒ   (2) ⓑ
(3) ⓐ   (4) ⓓ

3
(1) pen, hen   (2) ten, men
(3) wet, jet   (4) net, pet
(5) peg, leg   (6) red, bed

4
(1) ⓓ   (2) ⓐ
(3) ⓑ   (4) ⓒ

2 Short Vowels   pp 4,5

1
(1) sit, hit   (2) sip, lip
(3) pin, tin   (4) win, fin
(5) big, dig   (6) kid, lid

2
(1) ⓓ   (2) ⓑ
(3) ⓒ   (4) ⓐ

3
(1) hog, log   (2) dog, fog
(3) hot, pot   (4) box, ox
(5) job, sob   (6) hop, mop

4
(1) ⓐ   (2) ⓒ
(3) ⓓ   (4) ⓑ

3 Short Vowels   pp 6,7

1
(1) bug, hug   (2) gum, hum
(3) cub, tub   (4) fun, sun
(5) cut, nut   (6) cup, pup

2
(1) ⓓ   (2) ⓐ
(3) ⓒ   (4) ⓑ

3
(1) rat   (2) hen
(3) pit   (4) dot
(5) sub

4
(1) fat, rat   (2) wet, net
(3) sip, rip   (4) hit, pit
(5) fog, hog   (6) bug, rug

4 Short Vowels   pp 8,9

1
(1) bag   (2) pet
(3) pen   (4) tin
(5) log   (6) tub

2
(1) (b)at, (f)at   (2) (p)eg, (b)eg
(3) (f)in, (b)in   (4) (f)og, (h)og
(5) (p)ot, (d)ot   (6) (s)un, (b)un

3
(1) b(a)g, b(i)g   (2) p(a)t, p(i)t
(3) c(a)t, c(u)t   (4) f(a)n, f(u)n
(5) l(e)g, l(o)g   (6) r(i)b, r(u)b

4
(1) ⓒ   (2) ⓐ   (3) ⓔ
(4) ⓑ   (5) ⓖ   (6) ⓓ
(7) ⓕ

5 Short Vowels Review   pp 10,11

1
(1) cat   (2) bag
(3) jet   (4) peg
(5) dig   (6) fin
(7) dog   (8) fog
(9) nut   (10) run
(11) pit   (12) pot

2
(1) cat   (2) men
(3) log

3 bat-bag-rag-rat-mat-man-pan-mad-bad-cab-nap-hat

6 Consonant Combinations
pp 12,13

1
(1) block	(2) blast
(3) clap	(4) climb
(5) flag	(6) float
(7) plant	(8) plum

2
(1) ⓔ   (2) ⓒ   (3) ⓕ
(4) ⓐ   (5) ⓓ   (6) ⓑ

3
(1) clap	(2) plum
(3) flag	(4) plant
(5) black	(6) class
(7) clock	(8) flat

4
(1) clock	(2) block
(3) clap	(4) flag

7 Consonant Combinations
pp 14,15

1
(1) brick	(2) brag
(3) cry	(4) crab
(5) frog	(6) front
(7) grass	(8) grab

2
(1) ⓕ   (2) ⓓ   (3) ⓒ
(4) ⓑ   (5) ⓒ   (6) ⓐ

3
(1) cry	(2) grab
(3) frog	(4) brick
(5) brown	(6) crib

4
(1) frog	(2) brick
(3) crib	(4) grass

8 Consonant Combinations
pp 16,17

1
(1) sky	(2) skin
(3) small	(4) smell
(5) snow	(6) snake
(7) spot	(8) spin

2
(1) ⓐ   (2) ⓓ   (3) ⓕ
(4) ⓑ   (5) ⓔ   (6) ⓒ

3
(1) small	(2) spot
(3) snow	(4) smell
(5) snake	(6) skip

4
(1) spy	(2) smell
(3) skip	(4) snake

9 Consonant Combinations
pp 18,19

1
(1) glass	(2) glad
(3) sleep	(4) slow
(5) star	(6) step
(7) trcc	(8) trip

2
(1) ⓓ   (2) ⓕ   (3) ⓑ
(4) ⓔ   (5) ⓐ   (6) ⓒ

3
(1) trip	(2) glass
(3) tree	(4) stick
(5) start	(6) slip

4
(1) step	(2) glass
(3) slip	(4) tree

10 Consonant Combinations
pp 20,21

1
(1) ant	(2) tent
(3) jump	(4) lamp
(5) bank	(6) ink
(7) best	(8) fast

2
(1) ⓔ   (2) ⓕ   (3) ⓓ
(4) ⓑ   (5) ⓒ   (6) ⓐ

3
(1) ant	(2) lamp
(3) bank	(4) best
(5) bump	(6) sink

4
(1) tent	(2) jump
(3) ink	(4) fast

11 Consonant Combinations
pp 22, 23

1
(1) what
(2) wheel
(3) sheep
(4) shark
(5) chin
(6) chop
(7) thin
(8) thick

2
(1) ⓓ
(2) ⓖ
(3) ⓕ
(4) ⓑ
(5) ⓔ
(6) ⓐ
(7) ⓗ
(8) ⓒ

3
(1) what
(2) chop
(3) shark
(4) thick
(5) shirt
(6) three

4
(1) wheel
(2) thin
(3) chair
(4) sheep

12 Consonant Combinations
pp 24, 25

1
(1) fish
(2) wash
(3) lunch
(4) bench
(5) hand
(6) sand
(7) rock
(8) sick

2
(1) fish, dish, wish
(2) lunch, bunch, bench
(3) hand, band, sand
(4) rock, kick, sock

3
(1) fish
(2) lunch
(3) sand
(4) sick
(5) kick
(6) dish
(7) band
(8) sock

4
(1) fish
(2) lunch
(3) hand
(4) rock

13 Consonant Combinations Review
pp 26, 27

1
(1) class
(2) ink
(3) chin
(4) three
(5) sand

2
(1) wheel
(2) kick
(3) tent
(4) dish
(5) grass
(6) hand

3
(1) ⓒ
(2) ⓕ
(3) ⓑ
(4) ⓔ
(5) ⓐ
(6) ⓓ

4
(1) clock
(2) sand
(3) lunch
(4) front
(5) bump

14 Long Vowels
pp 28, 29

1
(1) cane
(2) mane
(3) lane
(4) plane
(5) play
(6) day
(7) bay
(8) hay
(9) rain
(10) pain
(11) brain
(12) train

2
(1) ⓕ
(2) ⓖ
(3) ⓑ
(4) ⓗ
(5) ⓒ
(6) ⓓ
(7) ⓐ
(8) ⓔ

3
(1) cake
(2) cane
(3) lane
(4) pail
(5) pain
(6) train
(7) day
(8) pay
(9) cape
(10) paint

4
(1) plane
(2) play
(3) hay
(4) rain

15 Long Vowels
pp 30, 31

1
(1) bee
(2) see
(3) three
(4) feet
(5) sheep
(6) meet
(7) sheet
(8) neat
(9) seat
(10) heat
(11) read
(12) tree

2
(1) ⓓ
(2) ⓐ
(3) ⓗ
(4) ⓒ
(5) ⓕ
(6) ⓑ
(7) ⓔ
(8) ⓖ

3
(1) bee   (2) see
(3) tree   (4) three
(5) feet   (6) meet
(7) sheet   (8) sheep
(9) seat   (10) heat
(11) neat   (12) read

4
(1) sheet   (2) tree
(3) read   (4) eat

16 Long Vowels
pp 32,33

1
(1) sky   (2) fly
(3) cry   (4) dry
(5) kite   (6) bite
(7) hike   (8) bike
(9) hide   (10) ride
(11) slide   (12) wide

2
(1) kite   (2) ride
(3) fly   (4) smile

3
(1) hide   (2) ride
(3) slide   (4) wide
(5) kite   (6) bite
(7) hike   (8) five
(9) cry   (10) sky
(11) fly   (12) dry

4
(1) bike   (2) slide
(3) five   (4) sky

17 Long Vowels
pp 34,35

1
(1) cone, bone   (2) coat, goat
(3) hose, rose   (4) float, boat
(5) nose, close   (6) toad, road

2
(1) ⓔ   (2) ⓑ   (3) ⓖ
(4) ⓓ   (5) ⓒ   (6) ⓕ
(7) ⓗ   (8) ⓐ

3
(1) cone   (2) bone
(3) rose   (4) nose
(5) hole   (6) rope
(7) coat   (8) goat
(9) float   (10) boat
(11) toad   (12) road

4
(1) coat   (2) boat
(3) rose   (4) nose
(5) toad

18 Long Vowels
pp 36,37

1
(1) cube   (2) tube
(3) cute   (4) flute
(5) tune   (6) dune
(7) blue   (8) glue

2
(1) cute   (2) cube
(3) tube   (4) tune

3
(1) cube   (2) tube
(3) cute   (4) flute
(5) tune   (6) dune
(7) blue   (8) glue

4
(1) dune   (2) glue
(3) flute   (4) cube

19 Long Vowels Review
pp 38,39

1
(1) make   (2) mail
(3) cone   (4) boat
(5) bee   (6) clean
(7) bay   (8) blue
(9) sky   (10) ride
(11) cane   (12) glue

2
(1) feet   (2) rain
(3) slide   (4) float

3
gate-date-name-nail-mail-maid-paid-
page-cage-cake-bake-wave-cave-lake-
plate-plane-cane-tail

1
(1) yk(hike)mpqt
(2) znth(blue)yx
(3) rt(meat)bidzu
(4) oprdy(road)wqs
(5) sqmdl(sheet)rty

2
(1) pl(a)n(e)   (2) sl(ee)p
(3) b(i)t(e)   (4) g(oa)t

3
(1) seat   (2) bike
(3) read   (4) tune
(5) cone   (6) rose
(7) cube   (8) hide

4
(1) blue   (2) boat
(3) slide   (4) cake

21 **Vocabulary**   pp 42,43

1
(1) one   (2) two
(3) three   (4) four
(5) five   (6) six
(7) seven

2
(1) two   (2) one
(3) seven   (4) five
(5) four   (6) six
(7) three   (8) two
(9) five   (10) one
(11) four   (12) seven

3
(1) d   (2) b   (3) e
(4) c   (5) a

4
(1) - (4) example answer

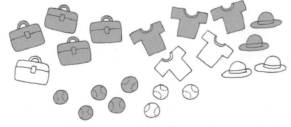

Above is an example answer. Answers will vary.
Make sure that 4 bags, 3 shirts, 2 hats, and 5
balls are filled in.

22 **Vocabulary**   pp 44,45

1
(1) wind   (2) leaf
(3) jump   (4) catch
(5) bird   (6) climb
(7) water   (8) wolf

2
(1) bird   (2) leaf
(3) climb   (4) wind
(5) catch   (6) water
(7) wolf   (8) jump

3
(1) d   (2) a
(3) b   (4) c

4
(1) bird   (2) jump
(3) catch   (4) wolf
(5) wind

23 **Vocabulary**   pp 46,47

1
(1) watch   (2) make
(3) glue   (4) string
(5) sing   (6) chair
(7) read   (8) desk

2
(1) string   (2) sing
(3) read   (4) chair
(5) watch   (6) glue
(7) desk   (8) make

3
(1) read   (2) chair
(3) sing   (4) watch
(5) make

4
(1) T   (2) F
(3) F   (4) T

24 **Vocabulary**   pp 48,49

1
(1) frog   (2) rabbit
(3) snake   (4) dog
(5) bat   (6) ant
(7) fish   (8) cat

2
(1) frog   (2) snake
(3) bat   (4) ant
(5) rabbit   (6) dog
(7) cat   (8) fish

3
(1) dog   (2) cat
(3) snake   (4) fish
(5) ant

4
(1) dog   (2) snake
(3) ant   (4) cat
(5) fish

25 Vocabulary
pp 50,51

1
(1) hot, cold   (2) new, old
(3) long, short   (4) fast, slow
(5) big, small

2
(1) new   (2) long
(3) cold   (4) fast
(5) old

3
(1) ⓐ   (2) ⓑ   (3) ⓑ
(4) ⓐ

4
(1) ⓓ   (2) ⓑ   (3) ⓔ
(4) ⓒ   (5) ⓐ

26 Vocabulary
pp 52,53

1
(1) left, right   (2) stop, go
(3) near, far   (4) up, down

2
(1) right   (2) left
(3) near   (4) far
(5) down   (6) up
(7) stop   (8) go
(9) right   (10) stop
(11) down   (12) near

3
(1) ⓐ   (2) ⓑ   (3) ⓑ
(4) ⓐ

4
(1)   (2)
(3)   (4)

27 Reading Comprehension
pp 54,55

1
(1) red   (2) sweet
(3) fox   (4) apples

2
(1) b   (2) a   (3) e
(4) d   (5) c

28 Reading Comprehension
pp 56,57

1
(1) T   (2) T   (3) F
(4) F   (5) T

2
(1) 5   (2) 4   (3) 2
(4) 3   (5) 1

29 Reading Comprehension
pp 58,59

1
(1) hair   (2) new
(3) black   (4) run

2
(1) c   (2) b   (3) e
(4) h   (5) a

30 Reading Comprehension
pp 60,61

1
(1) F   (2) F   (3) F
(4) T   (5) T

2
(1) 6   (2) 5   (3) 3
(4) 4   (5) 1   (6) 2

31 Reading Comprehension pp 62,63

1 (1) F   (2) T   (3) T
(4) T   (5) F

2 (1) hay   (2) pig
(3) hair, chin

32 Reading Comprehension pp 64,65

1 (1) stick   (2) stick
(3) pigs   (4) fell

2 (1) 6   (2) 2   (3) 5
(4) 1   (5) 4   (6) 3

33 Reading Comprehension pp 66,67

1 (1) When   (2) Who
(3) What   (4) Where

2 (1) paper, string   (2) pink
(3) red, K   (4) starts, with

34 Reading Comprehension pp 68,69

1 (1) F   (2) F   (3) T
(4) T   (5) T

2 (1) 5   (2) 2   (3) 4
(4) 1   (5) 3

35 Review pp 70,71

1 (1) sad   (2) rat
(3) hot   (4) sun
(5) tag

2 (1) ⓖ   (2) ⓑ   (3) ⓕ
(4) ⓒ   (5) ⓗ   (6) ⓓ
(7) ⓐ   (8) ⓔ

3 (1) pain   (2) read
(3) sheep   (4) sky
(5) bone   (6) tune

4 (1) lunch   (2) chair
(3) lake   (4) sleep
(5) fast

36 Review pp 72,73

1 (1) ① up, up   ② grass
③ stuck
(2) ① 2   ② 1   ③ 4
④ 5   ⑤ 3
(3) ① T   ② F   ③ T
④ T   ⑤ T